After the Ticking Stops

A collection of poems

by

Darien Belluomini

Copyright © 2014 Darien Belluomini

All rights reserved. This book or any portion thereof may not be reproduced or used in any manner whatsoever without the express written permission of the publisher. 5 bells Publishing, PO Box 7555, Chandler, AZ 85246.

Cover art/photo/design by Darien Belluomini

ISBN: 0692241205
ISBN-13: 978-0692241202
Library of Congress Control Number: 2014912903

Printed in the United States of America

First Printing, 2014

Through friendship, understanding, loyalty and shared love of writing and language, my deepest admiration and most sincere thanks goes to one of the best friends I have ever known, Jim "Buddy" Scott (James Edward Scott, Jr.). At the end of many conversations, he often used the phrase…"until the bitter end," to which I always replied…"and there is no end but that which is bitter." In his passing, I now know the truth and pain in these words. This book is dedicated to Jim, his memory and our writing. This is for you…

So now,

from knurled memoirs
and vacant suspicions
come the ramblings…
of days gone by,
days to come,
a thousand lifetimes,
and countless ruminations…

Table of Contents

To Go Again	1
Either	2
find me, please	3
At the Circus	4
Unaware	5
Dark	6
Story Time	7
Burned	8
Dissonance	9
Slight of Hand	10
"It" Is Comfort	11
Losing Track	12
It's Called Home	13
A Few Thoughts	14
Faces To See	15
Spinning	16
Jump	17
Some Thing	18
From Below	19
Self Portrait	20
Just Go	21
Directions…please?	22
Almost There	23
Riverboat	24
Over	25
…once, the noise stopped	26
Hope Misguided	27
Short Escape	28
Conversation	29
Cynicism	30
Waiting	31
Dead Lines	32
Fading Thought	33
How Wet is the Bottom of the Puddle	34
Precarious Assessment	35
Where It Goes	36
Here	37
Take Away	38
Wandering	39
For Shadow	40
Inattentively Navigating a Conspicuous Way Home	41
Looking For	42
Off the Floor	43
In the Tangles of Lace	44
The Incessant March	45
Within the Guise	46
Please Use Levity Instead	47
Make It Go Away	48
Put It on the Stone	49
Handcuffed	50
What It Means	51
Revisit	52
Opaque Performances	53
Where's My Bottle	54
Wayward	55
My Sea	56
Closed to Visitors	57
Unheard	58
A Walk In…	59
to be	60
Discover	61
Try Again	62

To Go Again

Malaise
Oh sweet malaise
How I need
To touch your face
How I want
Your sweet embrace
My thoughts will be
Of sweet malaise
And so my pen
Goes home to waste
Within the dreams
Of sweet malaise
Where rest my head
And sodden pace
To the clamorous song
Of sweet malaise
The beautiful sound
That leaves no trace
Does fill the mind
Of sweet malaise
While the heart
Is left to race
In malicious wait
Of sweet malaise
Please I beg
Remove the lace
It binds my hope
To this cruel place
This broken heart
Has stopped its chase
Please take my thoughts
Of sweet malaise

Either

Labeled

Intro

Weird

Bludgeoned with fear

Perverse

Wicked

Scenes

A day in the life, it seems

Philosophy

Logic

Insight

Push or jump, I might

Obscurity

Walking

Shoes

Profuse periods of blue

Fatigue

Grows

Cold

Into a darkness I go

AFTER THE TICKING STOPS

find me, please

i won't share it with you
you're not mine
i won't share it with you
it's not time
if i share it with you
my "alone"
then i've shared with you
my undertones

i want to share it with you
will you help me
i want to share it with you
i won't let you…

alone
with me
once more

i won't share it with anyone
my alone is mine to keep
i can't see what it's become
my alone is far too deep

i can give you some
but i'm afraid you'll run
so i'll share with none
my alone is done

i don't want it here
but i need it near
alone drives away
all that should stay

i want share it with you
not today

At the Circus

Upside out
Inside down
Twisted ways
Of a circus clown
Drawn emotions
Painted feelings
Silent words
So revealing
Disguise the face
Remain unseen
Be forgotten
Become routine

Unaware

Starting to see

The inner core

What things were planned

Forsake once more

Glances meet

In the middle where

Not much matters

Well, maybe a prayer

A different look

A brutal cry

Ominous tale

Distressing high

Obstructed views

Expose the void

Ever deeper

So much destroyed

<u>Dark</u>

Afraid of the dark

And all it brings

Creatures and monsters

And all those things

Afraid of the dark

A paranoid mind

Creating delusions

That surface entwined

Afraid of the dark

And under the bed

A quick flash of light

Is waking the dead

Story Time

Silently reciting
A novel of thoughts
With articulate prose,
Concepts and subplots

Silently devising
Through reticent stares,
Derisive inferences
And riddles they bear

Silently ciphering
The pensive resolve
Beyond the reach
Behind the walls

Silently masking
Constrained and tied
The secret study
Of a harsh divide

Burned

It looks the same
As the one before
And many others
Dammit, one more
Shall I go?
Now?
No
Again
Not allowed
Footprints expire
Don't look back
No shelter
Don't unpack
Never know
Who to believe
Already know
Who will leave

Dissonance

Pay attention
Now see here
Can't really feel
Without you near

Eyelids heavy
Uncertain mind
These new things
Are so unkind

Dearest heartbreak,
Your salty tears
Will never waive
Your spiteful years

disconnect

Reach for you
So far away
Don't know if you know
Still feel you every day

<u>Slight of Hand</u>

The way the words
Get to the page
Are simple muse
And not by sage

Mistake is made
To assume the real
When in the shadows
The muse does steal

Follow the rain
And darkened cloud
Find the muse
In a darkened shroud

Never be gone
Always confuse
Never a sage
The timeless muse

"It" Is Comfort

Another step
Lost the guide
Face the echo
Death inside
On display
Are guarded wares
Easier that way
It hurts to care
Comfort is
Familiar things
Regardless of
Sufferings
Frail bones
And feeble hearts
While one heals
The other departs
Familiar
Because it hurts
Don't mean it's good
Just means it works
And so it's set
Once again
Decision made
To break, not bend
So well hidden
Insides rot
Far too late
To make it stop

Losing Track

Vacant

Empty box

Wasted feeling

Ticking stops

All stands still

Pending frame

Twisted scenes

Drama stain

Carved by woe

Thinking stops

Walk the ruins

Paradox

It's Called Home

The gate that rattles
The fence that screams
These are noises
That haunt my dreams
Dry wind blows
Across my face
Same damned wind
Rattles that gate
Sun is hard
One eye closed
Bakes my skin
Unopposed
Nothing lives here
Not even a weed
Nor lowly bug
Nor statuesque tree
Call this home
My desolate place
Here too long
Wind burned face

A Few Thoughts

From an emotional indication
It's a cynic's incitation
From a cynic's observation
It's self-incarceration

Within one's own emotion
Is serene corrupt devotion
Within a single notion
Is diversified commotion

In time this great insanity
Affords a great calamity
In light this great duality
Affords a false indemnity

Faces To See

For here to cast

That burdened stare

The haunting look

That never cares

It matters not

Too young or old

When on the doorstep

Feet grow cold

Makes no difference

Foul or fair

He still rides

That fiery Mare

Last regard

In a somber view

Is to see the face

Of death so true

<u>Spinning</u>

Sober storm
Gripping fear
Who would listen
Who would hear
Cries are piercing
Illness is said
Simply exists
Inside your head
They won't see
But I feel
The sickened spinning
Of this God-damned wheel
Illness in tow
Unwanted guest
Angry storm
Praying for rest

Jump

So I may delve

My blackened room

Pictures dark

With light of gloom

Perched high above

The pompous deep

Found the thought

From which to leap

Tell the tales

The room below

Lies in wait

Let it go

Some Thing

Salts of burn
Tales of turn
Candidly chip away

Water that wears
Feelings that tear
Friends that truly betray

If not for the years
Or the weather of tears
Suffering wouldn't feel

They trip the start
They break the heart
Then life is what they steal

From Below

Blankets of dirt
Covered in stone
This fuckin' tomb
These fuckin' bones
Been laying here
For quite some time
So long in fact
I've lost my mind
No conversation
Nothing comes out
Brittle bones break
When I open my mouth
No visitation
Nothing comes near
Just worms and maggots
Gnaw on my ears
So this is the end
A good look at death
Things do not change here
So don't hold your breath

Self Portrait

Paint a picture
    Of the night

Tease it with
    Oil and light

To lose the sense
    Of that which be

Paint a picture
    That is me

Just Go

To know this ruse insane
Is to dance every day

To play with the pain
Is chaotic every day

To watch sunlight wane
Is comfort every day

To discover the end mundane
Is to fear every day

To torture this brain
Is torture every day

To interpret the arcane
Is maddening every day

To never explain
Is to blur every day

Run away

Run away

Every

Day

Directions…please?

The extraordinary nature
Of counter-productivity
Leans amicably over the edge
Of misguided ambiguity
So when the menial inference
Of patronizing soliloquy
Contains indignant reference
To perverse diseased serenity
It dons the guise erroneous
Of tempestuous bleak sobriety
And circumnavigates perception
To subsequent anonymity

Almost There

The glove drops
While the clock tick tocks
As time nonsensically bleeds away

The muse is taxing to know

Because he makes it that way
He'll get it right, someday
It's always grey
What not to say
Maybe today

Implicit windings
Are self-inflicted findings

The glove drops
While the clock tick tocks
As time irreverently burns to the floor

Introspection is cruel

Muse follows muse behind the door
And they are still broken
Same as before
Bent hands explore
The never more

Not enough space on the page
When disgrace is the standard gauge

The glove drops
While the clock tick tocks
As time carelessly fades

In shadows he hides
Covering only one eye
Wistfully muttering
A lonely goodbye

Riverboat

Locked away
Inside these walls
Rough and sterile
Psychosis falls
The white of black
Of true mundane
Never realize
Can't explain
The vehicle by which
This path will end
Sails the Styx
Your coin they'll send

AFTER THE TICKING STOPS

Over

To no avail
The perils within
Are all self-taught
And burrow the skin
Every slice
Dissevers divine
Paring flesh from
The heels of time
Breathe in deeply
Try not to choke
Drown in mourning
Too taxing to cope
Tongue grows thick
Covered in blame
Always at fault
Always the same
No cure prevails
So please, don't wait
There will always be
Foolish mistakes
A need exists
For a darker place
To consume remorse
In a lethal chase
Broken
Ruined
Exhausted sigh
Earned is deserved
Day goes by

...once, the noise stopped

in wasted days
and wasted ink
in wasted heads
is where we think
go back to
the bending of things
twist and knot
the broken seed
pretense is key
to silence concern
one mind in many
blank stare returns
sentiments untold
mirror grows old
noise unfolds
so cold

Hope Misguided

A wish is a wish
And merely such
If too many are made
Not one will touch

If none exist
Not one comes true
No plans maligned
No path askew

So what precludes
Decisions to wish
Is it want or need
Or tempt and anguish

What void we'll fill
Grows ever more
When wishes are made
And not explored

A wish is a wish
Obscure as a dream
Not one will touch
Not one foreseen

Short Escape

The aft and fore

Of sweet misery

Takes control

And permeates me

Wind and sand

May grind my hands

But a short escape

They make

Nothing can tame

The kneading of pain

The feel of hurt

Or the taste of dirt

So if in a moment

My head is clear

A grievous turn

Was already here

Conversation

Thinking alone
Thoughts of not
Think what comes
Alone in a plot
Sit and talk
With nary a host
Sitting alone with
A talkative ghost
Finding the logic
Typically veils
Finding the end of
The logical trail
While madness echoes
Moments are filled
By one silent voice
That is echoing still

Cynicism

Swimming in fiction
Pardon the masses
Momentary penance
To save their asses

Repent the wrongs
Repress and then
Seven more days
To sin again

Follow the words
Follow the act
Curtain goes up
Dichotomy of fact

Saddle of guilt
Sermon begins
Watch the leaders
Deliver their sins

Waiting

Fate has broken
Seals of four
Glint of light
Final score
Curving anguish
Springs disease
Beg forgiveness
On bended knee
Greed of want
For ever more
Peace removed
Impel the war
Food foregone
Brings hunger home
Greeted by
Skin and bones
Add to three
The ashen fourth
Cannot stop
This charging horse
Crimes of self
Destroy the mass
The end begins
A shadow cast

Dead Lines

Wake in a stir
Offer a cross
Vomit the fear
Dread of chaos
Truth destroyed
Misguided
Withheld
Impossible to know
What night will sell
Euphoric dysfunction
Suffer through sleep
Ambiguity
A dead line to keep

Fading Thought

Purple light
Neon sign
Drunken glow
Leave behind
Sullen words
Mark and slice
Covered eyes
Feel good vice
Fading view
Fading track
Fading breath
Fade to black
Rope is set
In this scene
Bind the hands
In this dream
Mind of words
Mouth of mute
Hide the years
Hold the truth

How Wet is the
<u>Bottom of the Puddle</u>

Turn the head
They won't see
Water and salt
Flow with ease

Now turn again
Feeling shame
Even tears can't
Paint over pain

Walk in a cloud
Sensing the stares
Stay well hidden
Wishful repairs

Turn once more
Hoping for hope
No way out
Draw in smoke

No place left
Now turn away
Trapped by a circle
The tears have made

Precarious Assessment

Habitual apprehension
Ill-timed compulsion
Critical self-admission
Mumbling deduction

Pontificating

Ridiculous profundities
Of perceived addiction
Strewn from a pen
With a deviant mission

Stuck in the grindings
Ideas to chase
Describing delusions
Another made-up place

Where it Goes

Listen
It's not there
Scare the scene
With rip and tear
Leading into
False fixations
Running from
Morose sedation
Feed the fix
Far and away
Fix the far
And fill the page
No escape
Happens tonight
The fix will fill
From quill of spite

Here

I used to know
A neat little boy
He was a simple kid
And he loved simple toys
A long while ago
He and I lost touch
And I'm afraid to admit
We don't remember much
Desperate to find him
Before the picture goes away
I know he's still around though
I've seen him run and play
Now I would barely recognize
His outlined silhouette
He's the ghost in a memory
Of that boy I can't forget
Neat little boy
Please, come back to play
I sure do miss you
Hope to see you again, someday

Take Away

Conceal the urge
To reach for more
Put out the fire
To seek and explore
Snuff the want
To take a chance
Remove the will
To dance the dance
Burn the need
For eager dreams
Repress the search
For simple things
Take away
With just one swing

Wandering

Half the hell

That walks with me

Inside my head

And faded screams

What breaks the glass

And stains the walls

Haunts my head

This shallow vault

Half the hell

That walks with me

Will never know

Will never see

Half this hell

Is half the hell I need

For Shadow

And so it goes
Lost in memory
Hands bound to feet
Frail apology

Brush my cheek
I frame your eyes
Break my heart
It's no surprise

These damned trails
They have no end
They torture dreams
They condescend

Burned by my
Obtrusive addictions
Directed by my
Intimate convictions

Enemies unknown
Voices unseen
Clues untouched
Malady serene

Inattentively Navigating a Conspicuous Way Home

The keystone
The path
The mined
The trap

A walk
In pain
Comfort
Disdain

The foundation
The lost
The vision
The cost

It comes
And goes
Never
Knows

The appearance
The mend
The learned
The penned

New
Worn
Ever
Torn

<u>Looking For</u>

Creeping tendrils
Of crawling fear
A path of paths
Does soon appear
A trail
Of left
To draw
A sketch
Things to be
Years go by
A step that bleeds
Thoughts awry
Center track
Thick of weed
Heart and soul
A pint of mead
The way of right
Must truly be
Of turning left
But where is me

Off the Floor

Forever not
For never more
Lying in remnants
Splintered floor

Of many vices
Pain seems best
Broken heart
Know the rest

Drifting away
Needing to rise
Caustic wounds
Succumb
Demise

Cannot repair
Cannot refuse
Romancing sorrow
No need to choose

In the Tangles of Lace

What to believe
Which way is mine
So many directions
What course resigned
Dark room desired
Safe place sought
Ghost of my genius
Guise often thought
Burden of sojourn
Forever, no home
Continue to wear
Continue to roam
A view obscured
A world endured
Still the child
Who wants to hide
And still be seen
And wants to know
Everything

The Incessant March

So the words may come

    Must repent
    Must confess
    Must be silent
    Must feel duress

So the words may come

    Feel the needle
    Feel the twitch
    Feel the want
    Feel the bitch

So the words may come

    See the real
    See the frail
    See the darkness
    See the veil

So the words may come
And they may bleed
And cause despair
And dire reprieve

Within the Guise

And in the masquerade

Of reverie divine
I find myself amused
Bereft
Devoid
Maligned

Ingest regret
Consume the source
Digest the anger
Convulse every course

Discolored is
The memory
Of blackened pain
That visits me

Reminds me of
Insanity
And all those things
That dance on me

But yet to know
What line to show
What tells the tales
That time unveils

Intimate with grief
Embrace the strange
Tease the edge
A fool's exchange

Please Use Levity Instead

Head in hands, again
Continue to write
Because the voice
Is tired, and trite
So spit this ink
On to the page
Mapping madness in
This fucking cage
Screams unheard
Silent voice
A nightmare with
No fucking choice
Persistence
Is worthless
Ends in gray
Must find
A better way
Empty
Cage
Empty
Page

Make It Go Away

The past is the now
…the current pain
…at present, disdain
…future bloodstain

Is it the now?
…has it passed?
…break it
…fast
…don't let it last

No, not now
…does it hold?
…a truth untold?
…no way to know

Then it whispered
…was it ever?
…the now or never?
…the question is, whether…

Put It on the Stone

Unsettling din
Gasping for wind
Repressing begins
Panic sets in

Just passed through
Won't be back
Reminders linger
Don't react

A dreadful caress
With sudden tensions
All felt helpless
No exceptions

Filth of closure
Memories fade
Scars remain
One more stray

Handcuffed

Strings into thoughts
Thoughts into knots
Thoughts not lost
Just strings
Strings and thoughts
Knots string thoughts
Strings and knots
Thoughts knot strings
Strings of thoughts
Not knots, just thoughts
Strings sting, not knots
Thoughts lost
Thoughts of strings
Just don't sting
Please knot
Just thoughts, not strings
Dammit, where are the knots
The sting
Of thoughts
From strings
To knots
Not strings, not thoughts
Not without knots
For the love of God
Where are thoughts lost
Please not knots
Please don't sting
Not thoughts
Please string to knots
Strings of thoughts
Don't sting
Please don't sting
They sting
The thoughts
That won't string
Into knots
For the love of God
Where are thoughts lost

What It Means

The blade of grass
The fallen tree
They do not know
What it means
The drop of rain
The empty stream
They do not know
What it means
Under the leaves
Hope is crossed
Somewhere love
Somewhere loss

Revisit

Coherence was
Falsely defined
Ran free too long
Failed by design
Identity crushed
So long ago
Wasted the years
Wreckage in tow
Well aware
But oblivious to
Repercussions without
Burdens of proof
False dreams led
While fate gave chase
And when they crashed
A violent embrace
Now the anguish
Of hiding despair
Pays back time
Its wicked share

Opaque Performances

Unclear deliberations
With no familiar fix
Show parasitic habitations
In petulant sterile conflicts

Misguided street fair plays
A poorly dressed charade
"Entrapments of the Norm"
The one-act masquerade

"Someday" eludes hailed notice
Silently hiding its face
In shadowed shelter bleeding
Its death belies this place

"Promise" gave itself away
To lonely souls misled
Never filled a single one
Exhausting days ahead

Anomalous tragic comedies
Unveil their scarred resplendence
Performing endlessly ad nauseum
For intimate feigned attendants

Where's My Bottle

Where's my bottle
Here's my pain
Where's my happiness
Heartbreak to gain
I've got a light
I've got my smoke
I've got my pain
On which to choke
Where's my bottle
The color is blue
Comfort is gone
A heart once knew
Broken glass
Heart shaped stain
Found a bottle
Here's my pain

Wayward

Don't stray from hope
Must stay the course
The beaten path
Is the beaten horse

The miles of ground
Before the sleep
Come quick ahead
As does the deep

The search to find
Reveals to some
But what is crude
And what is done

Repeat the norm
Again disgust
Same damned track
Lack of trust

My Sea

In this night

I see my sea

Demonic tides

That follow me

The way I find

It matters not

For all is lost

The dreamer's loch

Will the water

Bless the bough

Or crack the hull

Ship goes down

Either course

Renders spite

I see my sea

In blackened light

AFTER THE TICKING STOPS

Closed to Visitors

Fingertips cold
Alone in this chair
Pushed through the halls
Pressed by their stares

Wheeled to a closet
So haunting and cold
Astonishing terror
About to unfold

Hands,
now numb with fear
Feet,
now frozen to the chair
Mind,
now still with despair

Pernicious crown
Fictitious repair

Contemplations of dismay
Follow an eerie cliché
Of "forever and a day"
As light quickly fades

Other side, colder still
Senses, beaten and bare
Pain defies expression
Falling awake from the chair

<u>Unheard</u>

But not for now
Do these tears fall
But for next time
Do voices call
With eyes laced shut
Hopeless at rest
They call again
Stale comfort, at best
And while the view wanes
The difference is the same
But for now
It sounds insane
They scream my name
They scream my name
And the death of sound
Is the death of light
And the death of me
Returns every night

A Walk In…

In lieu of wake
This scene does make
Me try to find
My truth unkind

My search…
no fruit

My steps
… aloof

Where are the scissors
I have cuts to make
Where are my hands
The scissors can't take

I reach
I reach
But
As I draw ever near

The drawer

Defiantly

Disappears

It's a comical state
Of invisible wake
Where are those scissors

I have cuts to make

to be

it is anonymity

to stay behind

to remain silent

to not bother

to be awake

it is temporary

to be a shadow

to be disturbed

to strip identity

to remain hidden

it is weary

to be unread

to be unheard

to be invisible

to disappear

Discover

Freedom
Denied
Concede
Abide

Hysteria surely greets
Perils of the dark
Their hallowed voices wail
Ripping flesh apart

Wrathful daylight turns
Into the sleep of fear
That face is seen again
Dreams become severe

Awaken unknown creatures
Change corrupts the air
Terrify the curious
In short, the dark is fair

Commotion slowly ends
When chaos settles in
It brings about an order
Although it's paper thin

<u>Try Again</u>

hush hush

Don't cry

On the mend

Stand by

Unforeseen

Frame lapse

Try again

Thunder claps

Realize

In a rush

Sorrow is

hush hush

www.ingramcontent.com/pod-product-compliance
Lightning Source LLC
LaVergne TN
LVHW021622080426
835510LV00019B/2707